MINIBEASTS UP CLOSE

Ladybugs Up Close

Greg Pyers

Chicago, Illinois

Published by Raintree, a division of Reed Elsevier, Inc.
Chicago, Illinois
Customer Service 888-363-4266
Visit our website at www.raintreelibrary.com

For information, address the publisher:
Raintree, 100 N. LaSalle, Suite 1200, Chicago, IL 60602

09 08 07 06 05
10 9 8 7 6 5 4 3 2 1

Printed and bound in Hong Kong and China by South China Printing Company Ltd.

Library of Congress Cataloging-in-Publication Data

Pyers, Greg.
Ladybugs up close / Greg Pyers.-- 1st ed.
p. cm. -- (Minibeasts up close)
Includes bibliographical references and index.
ISBN 1-4109-1530-1 (hc) -- ISBN 1-4109-1537-9 (pb)
1. Ladybugs--Juvenile literature. I. Title. II. Series.

QL596.C65P94 2005
595.76'9--dc22
2004022292

Acknowledgments
The publisher would like to thank the following for permission to reproduce photographs:
APL/Ravo Images/Glen Ravenscroft: p. **28**; Auscape/John Cancalosi: p. **27**, /Jean-Jacques Etienne-Bios: p. **8**, /Pascal Goetgheluck: p. **14**, /C. Andrew Henley: pp. **10, 18, 19**, /OSF/Paulo de Oliveira: p. **15**; © Dennis Kunkel Microscopy, Inc.: p. **12**; Lochman Transparencies/Jiri Lochman: p. **6**; Dr. Russell F. Mizell: p. **29**; photolibrary.com: pp. **13, 20, 21, 24, 25**, /Animals Animals: p. **7**, /SPL: pp. **4, 11, 26**; © Paul Zborowski: pp. **5, 22, 23**.

Cover photograph of a seven spot ladybug reproduced with permission of photolibrary.com/SPL/C. Nuridsayn & M. Perrenou.

Every effort has been made to contact copyright holders of any material reproduced in this book. Any omissions will be rectified in subsequent printings if notice is given to the publisher.

Contents

Any words appearing in bold, **like this,** are explained in the Glossary.

Amazing Ladybugs!

Have you ever seen a ladybug? Perhaps you have seen one climbing up a plant stem. Maybe one has rested on your finger before opening its wings and flying away. When you look at them up close, ladybugs really are amazing animals.

If you look closely, you may see a ladybug in a garden.

What are ladybugs?

Ladybugs are **beetles.** They are small, round, and brightly colored. Most ladybugs are red or yellow, with black spots. But some are brown, and some have white spots. Some ladybugs have 7 spots, others have 14 or 22 spots.

This **species,** or kind, of ladybug has no spots.

Like all beetles, ladybugs are insects. Insects have six legs and no bones inside their bodies. Instead, their bodies have a hard, waterproof skin. This skin is called an **exoskeleton.**

Different names

In Australia and the United Kingdom, ladybugs are known as ladybirds.

Where Do Ladybugs Live?

Ladybugs live in all parts of the world, except Antarctica. Like all insects, ladybugs are most often seen when the weather is warm. But they can survive very cold winters.

Habitat

A **habitat** is a place where an animal lives. Different **species** of ladybugs have different habitats. In Great Britain, the orange ladybug lives only in forests. This is because it eats the **fungus** that grows on tree trunks.

This type of ladybug lives in rain forests.

Looking for warmth

In the fall, large numbers of ladybugs may come into houses. They are in search of shelter for the winter.

The water ladybug finds its food in wet, muddy places. The striped ladybug finds its food in pine forests. The two-spot ladybug lives in many habitats. This is because the insects it eats also live in many habitats.

Two-spot ladybugs are often found on tree trunks.

Ladybug Body Parts

A ladybug's body has three main parts. These are the head, the **thorax,** and the **abdomen.**

The head

A ladybug's head is much smaller than its thorax and abdomen. The head has two feelers called **antennae,** two eyes, and a mouth. The mouth has strong, biting jaws called **mandibles.**

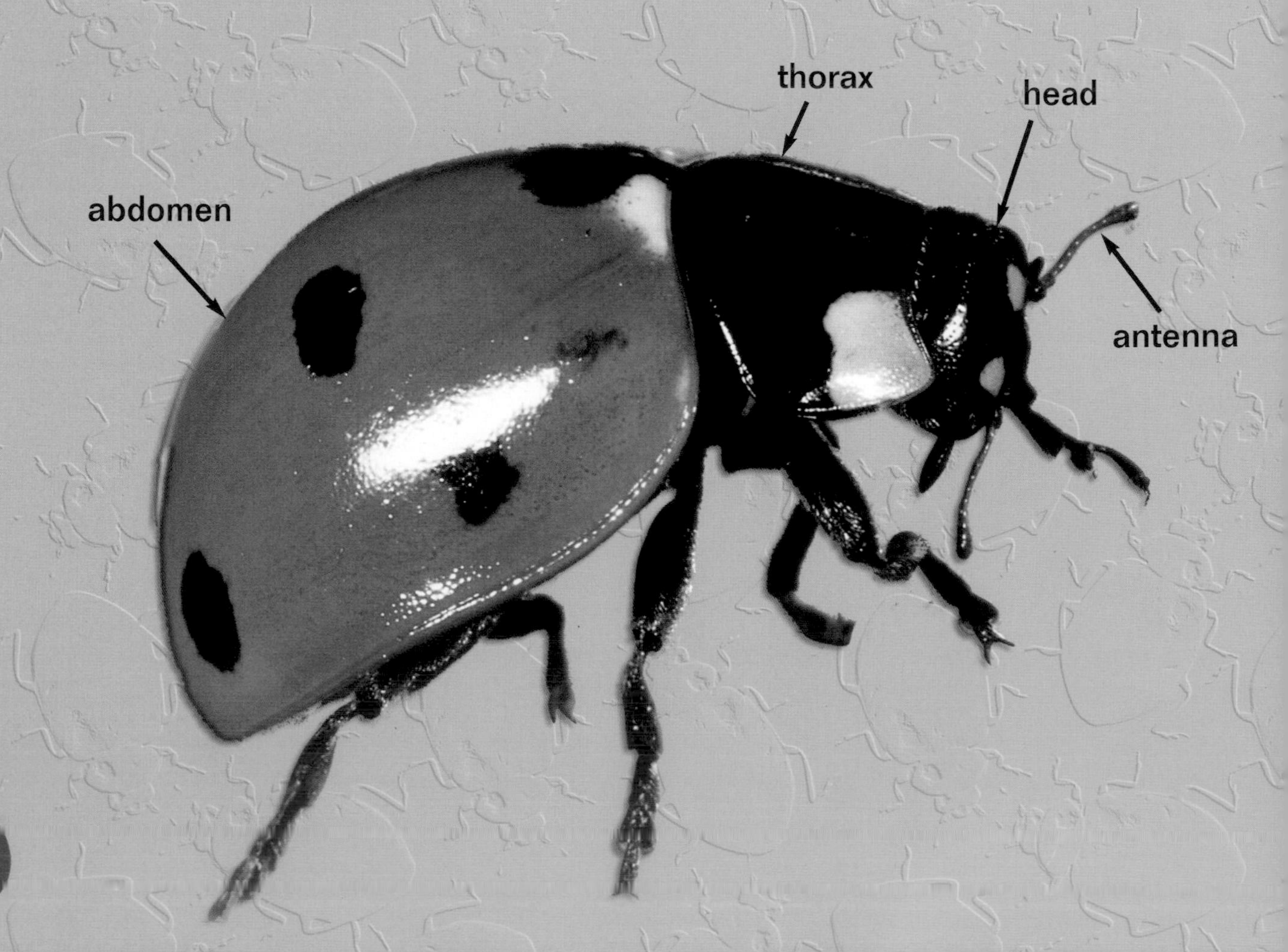

The thorax

A ladybug's wings and all six of its legs are attached to the thorax. There are strong muscles inside the thorax. These are needed to work the wings and legs.

The abdomen

Food is digested in the ladybug's abdomen. This means the food is broken down into tiny pieces. In females, eggs are produced in the abdomen.

Under cover

The ladybug's abdomen is usually completely covered by the wings. The abdomen can be seen only when the ladybug spreads its wings to take off.

Mouthparts and Eating

Most ladybugs eat small insects called aphids. Aphids are easy to catch because they move very slowly. When aphids are feeding, they do not move at all.

This ladybug is eating an aphid. Ladybugs also eat other small insects, such as scale insects.

Jaws

Ladybugs have strong jaws, or **mandibles,** which can easily crush the soft bodies of aphids. In its lifetime, a ladybug may eat more than 5,000 aphids.

Before they become adults, ladybugs are **larvae.** Larvae are tiny grubs, but they have strong jaws. One ladybug larva may eat 400 aphids before it begins to change into an adult.

Palps

A ladybug has **palps** on each side of its mouth. They help to move the food to the mouth.

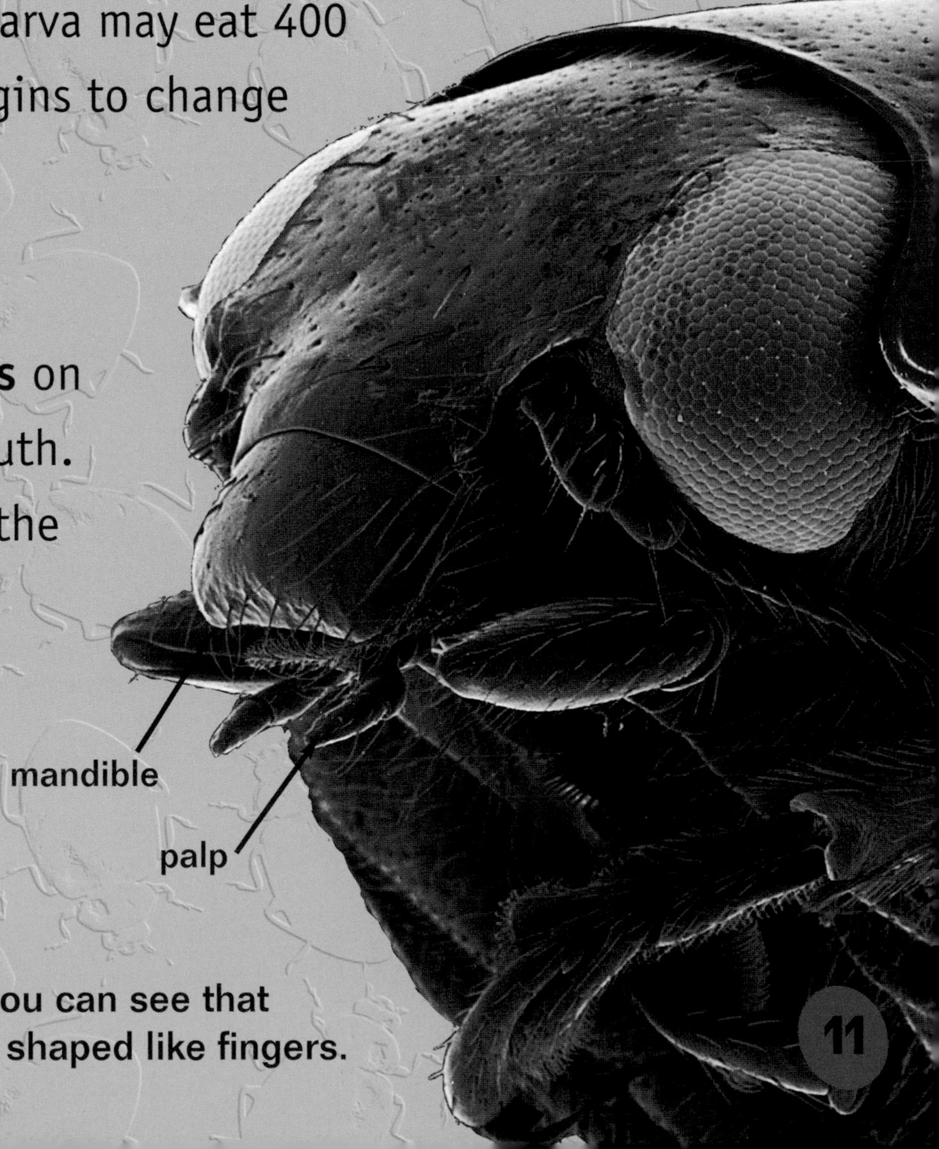

In this close-up photo you can see that the ladybug's palps are shaped like fingers.

Seeing and Sensing

Ladybugs can see, taste, and smell. But not in the same way we do.

Eyes

A ladybug has two **compound eyes.** Each compound eye is made up of thousands of very small eyes. Each small eye faces in a slightly different direction. Together, the small eyes give a ladybug an excellent view to the front, side, and back.

This close-up photo shows how the small eyes of a compound eye fit tightly together.

Antennae

A ladybug uses its **antennae,** or feelers, to smell. This helps the ladybug find its **prey** or a mate. The ladybug also uses its antennae to touch and taste.

The antennae can **sense** air movement. A sudden breeze may warn the ladybug that a **predator** is near. It might warn that a strong wind is coming, and that it should hold on tight or seek shelter.

Palps

A ladybug uses its **palps** to taste its food.

This ladybug is using its antennae to sense the air.

Wings and Flying

Ladybugs have two pairs of wings. But only one pair is used to fly.

Wings

The two front wings are really wing covers. They are hard and thick. They protect the rear pair of wings.

A ladybug's rear wings are its flying wings. They are thin, soft, and clear. When a ladybug is not flying, these wings are safely hidden beneath the wing covers.

A ladybug's wing covers are what you see when you look at its back.

Flying

Ladybugs fly to get away from **predators,** such as spiders. Another reason is to search for food. When a ladybug prepares to fly, it climbs to a high point on a plant. It folds its wing covers back, then unfolds its flying wings. These wings beat so fast they appear as a blur, and then the ladybug takes off.

wing cover

flying wing

This ladybug is about to land on a plant stem covered in aphids.

Fast wing beats

When flying, a ladybug's wings beat up and down between 80 and 90 times a second.

Inside a Ladybug

Ladybugs have blood that is clear and a heart that is a tube.

Blood

A ladybug's blood moves through the spaces in its body. The blood travels from the head, through the **thorax,** and into the **abdomen.** From there, the heart pumps it forward again.

How do ladybugs get air?

A ladybug does not breathe through its mouth. It gets air into its body through tiny holes called **spiracles.** These are on each side of a ladybug's body.

The brain

A ladybug's brain gets information that it **senses** through its **antennae,** eyes, and **palps.** It sends messages to the rest of the ladybug's body about what to do.

What happens to food?

When a ladybug swallows, pieces of food pass along a tube and into the stomach. As the food moves, it is broken down to release **nutrients.** A ladybug needs nutrients to stay alive. Waste passes out through the anus.

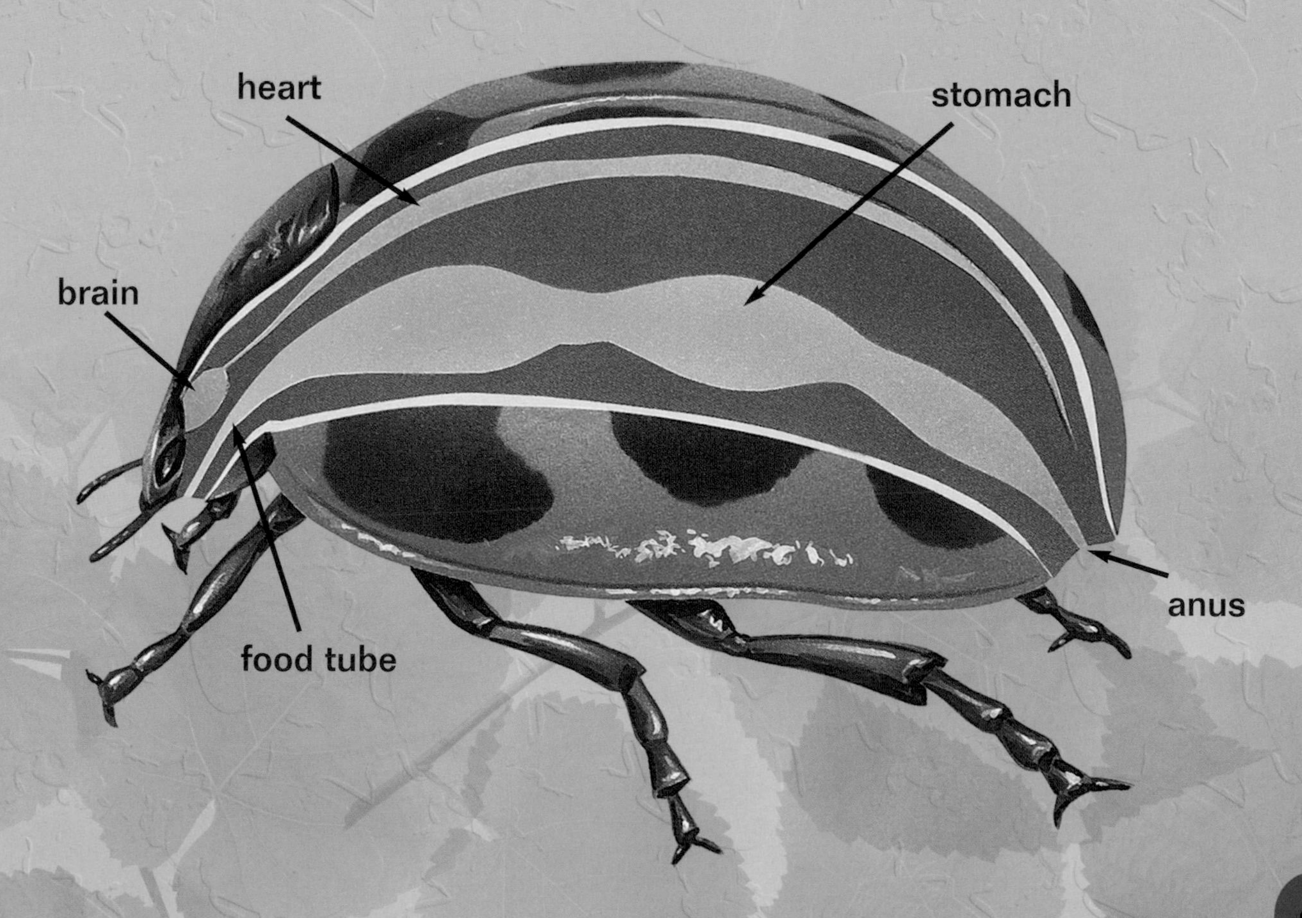

Eggs and Larvae

After she **mates** with a male, a female ladybug lays her eggs in the warm weather of spring and summer.

Eggs

The female lays between 20 and 30 eggs. She lays them on a plant where there are many aphids. The eggs stick to the leaf or stem in a tightly packed group. After a week, the eggs begin to hatch.

This ladybug has just laid her eggs on a leaf.

Ladybug larvae climb up and down stems and leaves looking for aphids to eat.

Larvae

Tiny grubs break through the thin eggshells and crawl from the eggs. These grubs are the ladybug **larvae.** The larvae eat their empty eggshells and then go in search of aphids to eat. A ladybug larva eats about 30 aphids a day.

A larva does not look like an adult ladybug. It has six legs, but it is a different color and has no wings. Its body has stiff hairs on it.

Becoming an Adult

A **larva** grows very fast. It soon outgrows its own skin. The skin splits and the larva crawls out in a new, bigger skin. This is called **molting**. The larva keeps eating and will molt several more times.

Pupa

Three weeks after hatching, the larva attaches its back end to a stem. Its skin then splits and falls off. What is left stuck to the stem is a **pupa**. An adult ladybug is growing inside the pupa.

This ladybug pupa is attached to a plant stem.

The adult

About a week later, the pupa's skin splits and an adult ladybug breaks out. It is soft and pale. It stays still on the stem while its **exoskeleton** hardens. In an hour it will be able to fly. In a day, its adult colors and spots will appear.

Breaking free

It may take a ladybug 30 minutes to break out of its pupa.

This California ladybug has just crawled out of its pupa.

Protection

A ladybug has many ways to protect itself from **predators.**

Ladybug defenses

A red and black ladybug is very easy to see as it walks up a green stem. However, predators learn that brightly colored insects have stingers or taste awful. Ladybug **larvae** and adults do not have stingers, but many of them have a horrible taste and smell. Once a bird, a spider, or a frog has tasted a ladybug, it will leave other ladybugs alone.

With their bright colors, ladybugs are very easy to see.

Larvae defenses

Ladybug **larvae** have strong jaws that can be used to fight off small predators, such as shield bugs.

Sometimes, when a predator is near, a ladybug will roll onto its back and pretend to be dead. Many predators will not attack an insect that does not move.

A ladybug can also tuck its head under the front of its **thorax.** Its feet act like suction cups. They hold the ladybug tightly to a stem or leaf so that a predator cannot pull it off.

This ladybug has tucked its head in for protection.

Ladybugs in Winter

When winter comes, there are no aphids. It is also too cold for ladybugs to move. So how do they survive?

Safe places

As the weather becomes cold, ladybugs find places that are dry and sheltered from the wind. This may be deep in the **leaf litter** of a forest, under bushes, or inside hollow logs.

These seven-spot ladybugs are sheltering together under a leaf for the winter.

Places to shelter

Ladybugs that live in pine forests may shelter among the pine needles high in a tree. Some ladybugs often shelter in cracks in the bark of tree trunks. Ladybugs also shelter in buildings such as garden sheds.

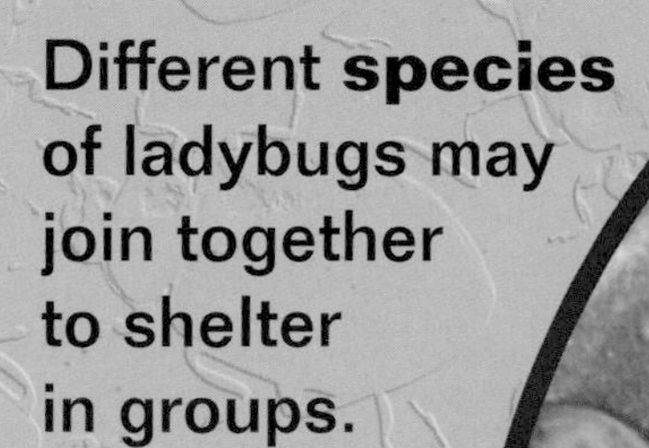

Different **species** of ladybugs may join together to shelter in groups.

Groups

Ladybugs often shelter in large groups. There may be hundreds or thousands of ladybugs in the same place. Some ladybugs return to the same place each winter.

By huddling in large groups, ladybugs are also using their own bodies as shelter. A chemical in their bodies keeps them from freezing. Ladybugs can even survive under snow when they are in these large groups.

Migrating Ladybugs

The convergent ladybug, a ladybug often found in the United States, travels, or **migrates,** many miles every year.

Getting warmer

In spring, in the valleys of central California, convergent ladybug **larvae** feed on aphids. By summer, these larvae will have become adults. But soon after, when it gets really hot, the number of aphids goes down. If the ladybugs stayed in the valleys, they would starve.

This convergent ladybug is eating aphids.

Time to move

In late summer, convergent ladybugs gather in huge **swarms.** There may be millions of ladybugs in a single swarm. They fly 50 miles (80 kilometers) or more to the mountains. It is cooler there and there is enough food to last until fall.

Getting colder

As winter comes, aphids disappear. The ladybugs rest over the cold months ahead. The following spring, the ladybugs **mate** and migrate back into the valleys. There will be aphids feeding on crops by then.

In winter, convergent ladybugs form large groups and shelter beneath logs and **leaf litter.**

Ladybugs and Us

Ladybugs are a sign of a good season for crops because they eat insects that damage crops.

Farmers' friends

Two Australian ladybug species were released in California more than 100 years ago. It was hoped they would control an insect pest called the cottony cushion scale insect. This insect attacks orange and lemon trees. The ladybugs saved the California fruit trees from disaster.

Many people like ladybugs.

Pests

When ladybugs seek winter shelter inside houses, they can be a real pest. If the ladybugs are disturbed, they give off a bad smell. In some parts of the United States, thousands of Asian ladybugs have been known to enter a single house to seek shelter for the winter. This ladybug was brought to the United States to control aphids.

Bean beetle

The Mexican bean **beetle** is a pest ladybug. It is brownish yellow with black spots. It feeds on bean leaves and pods.

These Asian ladybugs were removed from a house in the United States, where they went to seek shelter for the winter.

Index